Published in 2013 by The Rosen Publishing Group, Inc.
29 East 21st Street, New York, NY 10010

Weldon Owen Pty Ltd
Managing Director: Kay Scarlett
Creative Director: Sue Burk
Publisher: Helen Bateman
Senior Vice President, International Sales: Stuart Laurence
Vice President Sales North America: Ellen Towell
Administration Manager, International Sales: Kristine Ravn

Library of Congress Cataloging-in-Publication Data

Costain, Meredith.
 Ancient Egypt / by Meredith Costain.
     p. cm. — (Discovery education: ancient civilizations)
Includes index.
ISBN 978-1-4777-0051-8 (library binding) — ISBN 978-1-4777-0087-7 (pbk.) —
ISBN 978-1-4777-0088-4 (6-pack)
1. Egypt—Civilization—To 332 B.C.—Juvenile literature. I. Title.
DT61.C596 2013
932'.01—dc23
                                   2012019800

Manufactured in the United States of America

CPSIA Compliance Information: Batch #W13PK2: For Further Information contact Rosen Publishing, New York, New York at 1-800-237-9932

ANCIENT CIVILIZATIONS

ANCIENT EGYPT

MEREDITH COSTAIN

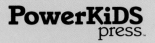

PowerKiDS press™

New York

Contents

Who Were the Pharaohs?

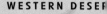

Alexandria
This fabulous city was planned by Alexander the Great.

Pharaohs were the most important and powerful people in ancient Egypt. They were the rulers, and the people who they ruled over believed that they were gods. The name pharaoh means "great house." According to Egyptian legend, in about 3100 BC, King Narmer (also known as Menes) is said to have united the two separate kingdoms of Upper Egypt and Lower Egypt to form a single great kingdom.

Since then, there have been many great rulers of ancient Egypt. Some of the most famous lived during the period known as the New Kingdom (1550–1070 BC), a time of great prosperity. Enormous temples were built at the Valley of the Kings in Thebes, the capital city, and at Abu Simbel.

Monuments of Giza
The pyramids and the sphinx are both famous landmarks.

WESTERN DESEF

Hatshepsut's temple
Queen Hatshepsut built a terraced temple beside the Nile.

Abu Simbel
Two huge temples were carved into the sandstone cliffs.

Queen Hatshepsut
Hatshepsut was one of the most successful pharaohs. Her name meant "foremost of noble ladies."

Akhenaton and Nefertiti
This royal couple, who lived at the city of Akhetaton, now known as Amarna, had six daughters but no sons.

Cleopatra
Cleopatra VII was the last descendant of Alexander the Great to rule ancient Egypt.

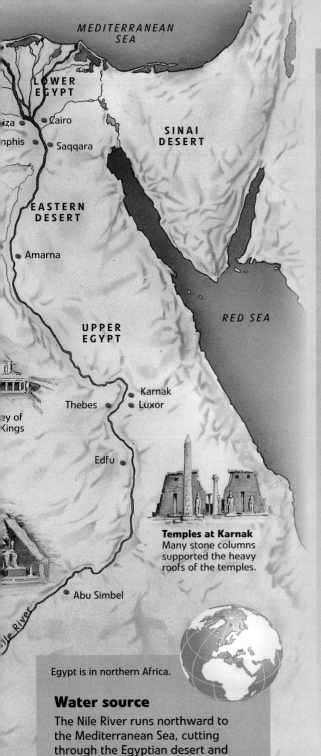

Temples at Karnak
Many stone columns supported the heavy roofs of the temples.

Egypt is in northern Africa.

Water source

The Nile River runs northward to the Mediterranean Sea, cutting through the Egyptian desert and providing water for its people.

RULERS OF ANCIENT EGYPT (1546–1070 BC)			
PHARAOH	**DATE OF DEATH** (circa)	**TOMB ENTERED**	**MUMMY FOUND**
Ahmose	1546 BC	not known	1881
Amenhotep I	1524 BC	not known	1881
Thutmose I	1518 BC	1824	1881
Thutmose II	1504 BC	not known	1881
Queen Hatshepsut	1483 BC	1824	not found
Thutmose III	1450 BC	1898	1881
Amenhotep II	1419 BC	1898	1898
Thutmose IV	1386 BC	1903	1898
Amenhotep III	1349 BC	1799	1898
Akhenaton	1336 BC	1817	not found
Smenkhkare	1334 BC	1907	1907
Tutankhamen	1325 BC	1922	1922
Ay	1321 BC	1816	not found
Horemheb	1293 BC	1908	not found
Ramses I	1291 BC	1817	not found
Seti I	1278 BC	1817	1881
Ramses II	1212 BC	1913	1881
Merneptah	1202 BC	1903	1898
Amenmeses	1199 BC	1907	not found
Seti II	1193 BC	1909	1898
Siptah	1187 BC	1905	1898
Queen Tausert	1185 BC	1909	not found
Setnakht	1182 BC	1909	not found
Ramses III	1151 BC	1768	1881
Ramses IV	1145 BC	open	1898
Ramses V	1141 BC	1888	1898
Ramses VI	1133 BC	1888	1898
Ramses VII	1126 BC	open	not found
Ramses VIII	1126 BC	not known	not found
Ramses IX	1098 BC	1888	1881
Ramses X	1098 BC	1902	not found
Ramses XI	1070 BC	1979	not found

Top to bottom

The king and the royal family were at the top of the social pyramid. At the bottom were prisoners of war, criminals, and slaves.

Royal family

Egyptian Social Order

Ancient Egypt had a very fixed social order, which was shaped like a pyramid. People believed that the gods gave them their various positions in society. At the very top was the pharaoh—the king, or occasionally the queen—who was believed to be the only living person able to communicate with the gods. The pharaoh was in charge of the army, the administrative service, and the priesthood. He or she was assisted by the educated upper classes.

Scribes and officials were well respected because they could read and write. Craftspeople came much lower down in Egyptian society. Below them was the largest group of people, the peasants, who grew food and worked as laborers on the royal buildings.

Did You Know?

Ancient Egyptians measured their wealth in cattle rather than money. Cows were counted every year and they were used to pay taxes.

Educated elite

Middle classes

Skilled laborers

The market
It was possible to buy many different goods, including all kinds of household items and food, in the marketplace.

Peasants and manual workers

THE SOCIAL PYRAMID

The number of people and the social structure of ancient Egypt varied across the centuries. These days, governments find out information about the people of their nation by conducting a census. But no census of ancient Egypt exists, so historians figure out the likely population numbers by counting the tombs and graves in various areas.

Educated literate elite, including the royal family: 5% of the population

Middle classes: 10–15% of the population

Peasants who worked the land: 80–85% of the population

At Home in Egypt

Most people lived in villages, in sun-baked mud-brick houses that were crammed close together. The houses had square rooms with small windows, and flat roofs, which were often used for cooking or, during the summer months, for sleeping. The average Egyptian home consisted of a central room, where the family spent most of their time, and three smaller adjoining rooms. Peasants lived in more basic dwellings consisting of only one windowless room. Cattle and goats were kept in a walled-in courtyard at the front of the house.

The rich lived in grand houses on spacious estates on the outskirts of the cities. Their homes often had flower gardens, fishponds, servants' quarters, granaries, stables, and a small shrine for private worship.

A tomb–worker's house

The royal tomb-builders who worked in the Valley of the Kings lived with their families in four-room houses. Made of stone and mud brick, the houses were designed to stay cool in summer.

Wall shrine
Ancestors and local gods were worshipped at wall shrines.

Window
High windows let the light in but kept the heat out.

Entrance
A thick stone wall stopped strangers from going inside.

Reception room

Narrow passageway

WEALTHY FAMILY'S VILLA

The homes of wealthy merchants and officials were spacious and comfortable. These villas had high ceilings supported by ornately decorated columns, barred windows, tiled floors, and walls painted with bright animal and plant designs. A staircase led up to the flat roof, which overlooked the peaceful gardens and pools filled with fish or the palm groves of their estate. The roof was also the coolest place to relax on hot evenings. Furniture was very simple—stools, low beds, and small tables were the most common pieces.

A rich Egyptian family relaxes at home.

Family room

Extra space
Extra rooms could be set up on top of the flat roof.

Oven
An oven made of mud bricks was used for baking bread.

Bedroom

Kitchen

Storage area
The basement area stayed cool, so it was used for storing food.

Rural Life

Most of the people of ancient Egypt were farmers, whose lives followed the cycles of the Nile River. Very little rain fell in this part of the world, and it was hot all year round. But every year, from July to October, the Nile burst its banks and flooded the fields on the surrounding river plain.

This was *akhet*, the time of flood and the season of rest. Farmers used this time to repair their tools, and peasants, who could not work in the fields, often worked on royal building projects. Next came *peret*, when the floodwaters subsided, leaving fertile black soil in the fields. This was the time for plowing fields, sowing crops, and building new irrigation channels. The third season was *shemu*, the time of harvest. Everyone worked hard to bring in the crops before the next cycle began.

The time of flooding
From July to October, the Nile swelled and burst its banks, flooding the fields and giving farmers time for rest and repairs.

A K H E T

Following the seasons
Egyptian farmers worked with the cycles of the Nile as it rose and fell. The flooded soil was made so rich by the nutrients and silt the floodwaters left behind, farmers never needed to use fertilizers.

Scattering seed

Sowing the crops
As the floodwaters of the Nile retreated, farmers scattered seed and plowed it into the fertile soil before the ground hardened.

P E R E T

Farmer plowing the soil

Plow   Hoe

Farm tools
Farmers used wooden hoes pulled by
oxen for heavy digging and for moving
the soil around. Light wooden plows
turned the soil easily.

FISHING

Besides being a highway for transportation and
trade, the Nile was also a source of food. Fish were
either harpooned, caught with hooks and lines, or
scooped up in nets made from papyrus. The marshes
bordering the Nile were home to ducks, cranes, and
other birds, which hunters caught in traps.

Houses safe from
floodwaters

he Nile floods fields.

Farmers
harvesting crops

Wheat and barley
for making bread
and beer

Bountiful harvest
The fertile silt deposited by
the annual floods resulted in
healthy crops of wheat,
barley, flax, fruits, and
vegetables for farmers.

S H E M U

The Afterlife

Ancient Egyptians believed that if they led a good life in this world, they would be rewarded after death. They would then make a journey into another world called the afterlife. Here, they would live with Osiris, the god of the dead, in the Field of Reeds. At first, the Egyptians believed that only the pharaoh had a soul strong enough to leave the tomb, travel to the afterlife, and live with the gods. During the Middle Kingdom (2040–1640 BC), these ideas changed, and people believed that observing the correct rituals after a person died would help that person journey to the afterlife.

Mourners were hired to weep and cover their head with dust at funerals. A priest performed the Opening of the Mouth ceremony at the tomb door, touching the face of the mummy with sacred tools. This allowed the deceased's soul to come back to life. After journeying to the west, the soul passed through a maze and answered questions. The final judgment came from Osiris himself.

Valley of the Kings
The valley's remote location made it less likely that the tombs built here would be plundered by grave robbers.

Canopic chest
The deceased's name was inscribed on the canopic chest and also on the coffin.

Worldly goods
Servants carried furniture, clothes, jewelry, games, and other items the deceased would need in the afterlife.

Nourishment
Food and drink were included in the procession so the spirit would have nourishment in the tomb.

THE *BOOK OF THE DEAD*

The *Book of the Dead* was a guidebook for the afterlife. Instructions on how to behave were written on the walls of a deceased person's tomb or on a papyrus scroll. The guidebook contained spells to help the person please the gods and prevent misfortune, as well as giving an overview of what would happen after death.

One man's journey
These paintings show the various stages of entering the afterlife.

Funeral procession

Mourners gathered at the home of the deceased to begin the long procession to the tomb. They dragged the mummy over land on a wooden sled, then crossed the river by barge.

Funeral bier
The mummy lay on a funeral bier protected by effigies of the gods.

Ritual ceremonies
Priests walked alongside, sprinkling purifying water and burning incense.

Transportation
Oxen pulled the sledge that carried the coffin through the desert.

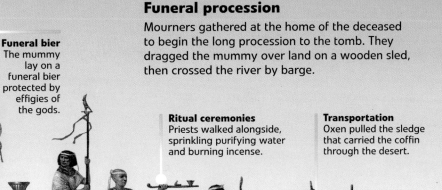

1. Washing the body
The body was cleaned with sweet-smelling palm oil or water, then moved to the *wabet*, the place of embalming. The embalming table was sloped so body fluids could drain away.

2. Removing the brain
The brain was pulled out through the nose with a bronze hook and thrown away. Sap was pushed into the skull cavity to stop bacteria from growing inside.

Mummification

A mummy is a preserved body. The ancient Egyptians were interested in finding a way to preserve bodies so their souls could live forever in the afterlife. They noticed that the skin of bodies that had been buried in the hot desert sands dried out and became hard and leathery. Without moisture, the bacteria that cause decay could not survive, and so the bodies did not rot.

The Egyptians copied this natural process that would preserve a body through their practice of embalming, or mummification. The elaborate procedure was carried out by priests and took about 70 days. The wealthy Egyptians continued the practice of mummifying their dead for the next 3,000 years.

ANIMAL MUMMIES

The ancient Egyptians mummified animals as well as people. At times, pets were made into mummies so they could join their owners in the afterlife. Mummies of animals that were sacred, such as crocodiles and cats, were offerings to the gods. They were buried in special animal cemeteries attached to temples.

Mummified crocodile

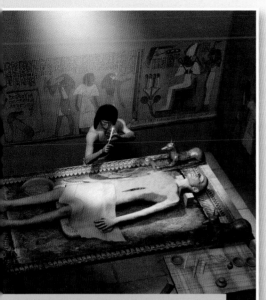

. Removing the organs
long slit was made in the left-hand side of
e body by a "slicer priest." The lungs, liver,
:omach, and intestines were removed and
reserved. The heart was left in the body.

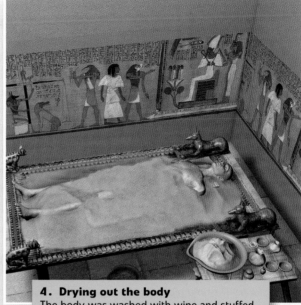

4. Drying out the body
The body was washed with wine and stuffed
with linen cloth, then covered with natron and
left for 40 days. Natron is a salt found on the
edges of salt lakes. It dried out the body.

. Initial wrapping of the body
he head was the first part of the body to be
vrapped in linen bandages. Jewelry and lucky
harms were wrapped with the body, and it
vas then bound in a linen sheet.

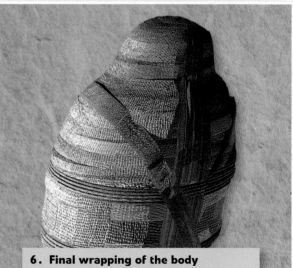

6. Final wrapping of the body
A final outer layer of linen completed the
wrapping process. Sometimes, a gilded mask
was placed over the mummy before it was
placed in the coffin.

Building the Pyramids

The Old Kingdom (2649–2150 BC) is known as the Age of Pyramids. Pyramids were enormous tombs, built to protect the mummified bodies of pharaohs for eternity. Each pyramid had a burial chamber deep inside it, surrounded by chambers containing goods the pharaoh would need in the afterlife. Early pyramids were a series of stepped platforms, so the pharaoh could climb the giant stairway to the heavens to join the Sun god Ra. Later pyramids had smooth, sloping sides, which formed a ramp for the pharaoh's journey.

Building pyramids was a time-consuming, difficult, and dangerous job. Many laborers crushed or broke bones, or slipped and fell to their death. They believed, however, that this work would give them a share in the pharaoh's afterlife.

Stone rolling

One theory for how laborers managed to haul massive stones across the desert was by using smooth wooden rollers coated with fine mud. Each stone was as heavy as a male hippopotamus.

TRANSPORTING STONE

There are many theories to explain how the pyramids were built. Most Egyptologists believe that canals, ramps, and shadoofs were used.

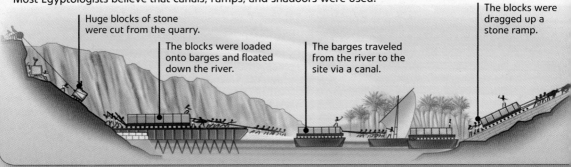

Huge blocks of stone were cut from the quarry.

The blocks were loaded onto barges and floated down the river.

The barges traveled from the river to the site via a canal.

The blocks were dragged up a stone ramp.

The Great Pyramid at Giza
A marvel of precision engineering, the Great Pyramid was built in 2551–2528 BC. It was the tomb of the 4th Dynasty pharaoh Khufu.

King's chamber
The king's chamber was the only one to be completed in the pyramid.

Queen's chamber
The purpose of the queen's chamber is still not known.

Underground chamber
This subterranean chamber was never finished, and its purpose is unknown.

Limestone casing
The limestone casing that once covered the pyramid has now been removed.

Grand gallery
A sloping corridor lined with polished limestone leads to the king's chamber.

Burial chamber

The smooth yellow walls of the burial chamber were covered with paintings. Inside the stone sarcophagus were three gilded coffins, one inside the other. The last coffin contained the mummy of Tutankhamen. Finding this golden shrine after so many years was a dream come true for Howard Carter.

Death mask
Tutankhamen's death mask was spectacular. It was made of solid gold inlaid with blue lapis lazuli.

Tutankhamen's Tomb

King Tutankhamen, known as the Boy King, began his rule when he was only eight years old. He died in 1344 BC, when he was eighteen years old. His resting place was discovered in 1922 by Howard Carter, and it is the only pharaoh's tomb not to have been badly looted. Even though it had been robbed at least twice before Carter discovered it, it was full of magnificent treasures—gilded statues, model boats, weapons, and chariots. Each item helped ensure Tutankhamen's safe passage to the afterlife.

Compared with other royal tombs, Tutankhamen's tomb was small, with only one entrance corridor and four chambers. Historians think that because Tutankhamen died suddenly when he was quite young, there was not enough time to build him a royal tomb. Instead, he was buried in a tomb meant for a nobleman.

Tutankhamen's gold funeral mask

Final coffin
The third and final coffin was made of solid gold. It contained the Boy King's mummy.

HOWARD CARTER

Howard Carter was an English artist and archaeologist. After five years of searching, he finally discovered the tomb of Tutankhamen on November 4, 1922. It then took him another 10 years to remove all of the treasures he had found from the tomb. Carter later became an agent for collectors and museums. He died in 1939.

Carter carefully cleans the pharaoh's third coffin.

Temple Complex at Karnak

Thebes became the capital city of Egypt during the New Kingdom (1550–1070 BC). Many grand temples were built, with the greatest of them at Karnak, near Thebes. This complex was dedicated to the worship of the god of the empire, Amen, his wife Mut, and their son Khonsu. Each of them had a precinct, or special area, in the complex. There was also a precinct for Montu, the falcon-headed local god.

Construction began in the sixteenth century BC and continued for 2,000 years, with a chain of pharaohs adding their own touches: for example, a new temple, shrine, or pylon carved with inscriptions. Most of the stone for this massive building project was brought to Thebes by boat from sandstone quarries in southern Egypt.

Pylon Two
A huge statue of Ramses II stood in front of the second pylon.

Boat shrine
This platform held the sacred boat of the god Amen.

Pylon One
The first pylon, or gateway, to the temple complex had flagpoles.

Sphinxes
An avenue lined with two rows of ram-headed sphinxes leads up to the first gateway, Pylon One. This avenue was built by Ramses II.

Obelisks
Standing stones were dedicated to Amen by Thutmose I and Thutmose III.

Pylon Three
The third pylon led to the entrance of the original temple.

Sanctuary
The original temple sanctuary of the god Amen has been fully restored.

Festival temple
Thutmose III's temple had columns shaped like tent poles.

Sacred lake
Temple priests purified themselves in the lake before performing rituals.

Pylon Eight
Queen Hatshepsut ordered this gateway to be built.

Great Hypostyle Hall
The hall contains 134 columns arranged in 16 rows. A roof would have rested on them.

Bark station
This chapel housed the sacred boat, or bark, of Amen.

Pylon Seven
This gateway was another element that Thutmose III added.

The Great Hypostyle Hall
The hall, containing a "forest" of huge columns carved with hieroglyphs, is one of the greatest works of architecture from ancient Egypt.

Temples and shrines

The Karnak temple complex covers 247 acres (100 ha) and is one of the most impressive sites in Egypt. It is made up of four main shrines: the Precinct of Amen, the Precinct of Montu, the Precinct of Mut, and the Temple of Amenhotep IV. There are also many smaller chapels, pylons, columns, obelisks, and sphinxes.

Abu Simbel

Ramses II, also known as Ramses the Great, built two temples at Abu Simbel, in what was then Nubia, a neighboring territory of Egypt. Ramses built the temples there to remind the Nubian people of his importance and also of his reputation as a great warrior king.

The smaller of the temples was decorated with statues of the king and his favorite wife, Nefertari. It is known as the Smaller Temple and was dedicated to Hathor, the goddess of love. The Great Temple was cut deep into the rock of a sandstone cliff. It contained a series of pillared halls and a sanctuary. The walls were decorated with paintings showing Ramses II riding into battle on his fine chariot. When the Aswan High Dam was built in the 1960s, the Smaller Temple, the Great Temple, and part of the cliff face were moved, piece by piece, to save the temples from the rising dam waters of Lake Nasser.

Entrance statues
Four colossal statues of Ramses II sit on either side of the temple entrance.

Sandstone cliff
The temple is cut 160 feet (48 m) into a steep wall of sandstone.

RAMSES II

Ramses II was one of Egypt's most powerful pharaohs, ruling for 67 years and having more buildings, temples, and statues built in his honor than any other pharaoh. He claimed the god Amen was his father and built Abu Simbel to boast of his own godly status. One of the statues in the sanctuary is of him.

The Great Temple of Ramses II at Abu Simbel

Entrance
A flight of stone steps leads to the entrance and the series of halls and sanctuary beyond.

Temple sanctuary

The innermost shrine of the Great Temple contains four seated statues of highly revered gods. Twice a year, on February 22 and October 22, the first rays of the Sun shine down the entire length of the hall and into the sanctuary, lighting up the statues.

Hypostyle hall
The hypostyle hall penetrates deep into the cliff and is supported by eight huge Osirid pillars, four on either side.

Sanctuary
This holds seated statues of four gods—Amen, Ptah, Re-Horakhty, and Ramses II.

Entrance hall
Eight large statues line the temple entrance hall, which leads to the temple sanctuary. The statues are of Ramses II in the form of Osiris, the god of the dead.

Egyptian Art and Culture

The ancient Egyptians created many fine works of art, including wall paintings, statues, pottery, and jewelry. Art was seen as an essential part of architecture and even of life itself. The artists who decorated the walls of the royal tombs were respected as master craftsmen. Jewelers worked with gold, silver, and a range of semiprecious stones to create necklaces, bracelets, rings, and earrings for both men and women. Stoneworkers created statues and vessels from hard and soft stones. Carpenters created ships, coffins, and fine furniture inlaid with ebony and ivory.

The walls of Egyptian tombs and temples were inscribed with picture writing, called hieroglyphs. Musicians entertained guests at private banquets and religious festivals, and dancers performed at funeral services. Musical instruments of the time included harps, lutes, pipes, rattles, and tambourines.

Plasterer
Plasterers made the wall smooth by applying a coat of plaster.

Scribes
Outline scribes transferred the sketched designs onto the wall with black paint.

A		I		Q		Y	
Vulture	Arm	Reed		Hillside		Double reed	
B		**J**		**R**		**Z**	
Foot		Snake		Mouth		No "Z"	
C		**K**		**S**	Door bolt	**CH**	
No "C"		Basket		Fold of cloth		Ropes	
D		**L**		**T**		**KH**	
Hand		Lion		Loaf		Placenta	
E		**M**		**U**	Quail chick	**SH**	
Reed		Owl				Lake	
F		**N**		**V**			
Horned cobra		Water		Horned cobra			
G		**O**		**W**	Rope coil		
Pot stand		Lasso		Quail chick			
H	Red hut	**P**		**X**			
Twisted flax		Stool		No "X"			

Musicians of the royal harem
The women of the royal harem were talented musicians and dancers. They played, sang, and performed to entertain the king.

Hieroglyphic "alphabet"
Hieroglyphs were arranged in rows or columns, and they could be read either from left to right or from right to left.

Egyptian art

Ancient Egyptian art told stories about people's lives and about the things that they expected to happen to them in the afterlife. Artists painted detailed scenes on houses, temple pillars, and tomb walls. There were strict rules about the way figures and objects could be shown.

Stonemason
Stonemasons carefully chipped out the main figures from the background wall.

Painter
Painters applied color to the base paint and used this to fill in the background details.

PAPYRUS

Papyrus was a plant that grew along the banks of the Nile. The reeds were used to make a thin material, also called papyrus, which was an early form of paper. River rafts were built from papyrus stalks, and boat rigging was made from twisted fibers. Papyrus was also woven and made into footwear and household goods.

Papyrus chest

Woven basket

Sandals

Scribe school
It took as long as 10 years for student scribes to memorize the hundreds of different hieroglyphic signs.

Discovering the Past

We can find out more about life in ancient Egypt by visiting its treasures in museums or reading writers of the past. For example, Herodotus, considered the first historian, described his visit to Egypt during the 27th Dynasty.

Egyptologists have also found a wealth of information by studying monuments and paintings and the things that the ancient Egyptians threw away. They have decoded records of daily events from hieroglyphs carved into stone or written on papyrus. Today, the people living along the Nile still employ many farming methods and tools used in ancient times.

Foreign excavatio

In 1816, Giovanni Battista Belzoni employed Egyptia workmen to drag the gia head of a broken statue of Ramses II from Thebes to the Nile. The head is currently on display in th British Museum in Londo Today, however, foreign excavators are no longer permitted to remove treasures from Egypt.

1798
French scholars arrived in Egypt with Napoleon's troops.

1799
The Rosetta stone was discovered by a French soldier.

1816
Giovanni Belzoni began collecting pieces for the British Museum.

1822
Linguist Jean-François Champollion decoded hieroglyphic script.

1858
National Antiquities Service was set up in Egypt.

The Rosetta stone
The discovery of the Rosetta stone enabled scholars to decode the meaning of hieroglyphs. It contained the same information in three different scripts.

TREASURE STORES

Museums around the world hold artifacts from ancient Egypt. The British Museum in London has coffins and mummies, as well as furniture, fine jewelry, and other burial items. The Cairo Museum in Egypt has a range of objects from Tutankhamen's tomb. In New York City, the Temple of Dendur has been rebuilt, stone by stone, in the Metropolitan Museum of Art.

Museum exhibits
Ancient Egyptian mummies and coffins are popular displays in museums all over the world.

80	**1922**	**1939**	**1992**	**1990s**
nders Petrie arted to survey e Great Pyramid.	Howard Carter discovered the tomb of Tutankhamen.	Pierre Montet discovered the royal tombs at Tanis.	The underwater survey of ancient Alexandria began.	CAT scans and DNA testing of mummies became possible.

Glossary

afterlife (AF-ter-lyf) A perfect existence after death in a perfect version of Egypt.

burial chamber (BER-ee-ul CHAYM-bur) A room where bodies are buried.

canopic chest (kuh-NO-pik CHEST) A wooden box containing jars in which the preserved organs of a dead person were put. The chest was usually placed in the tomb with the mummy.

census (SEN-sus) A process of obtaining information about a population.

chariot (CHAR-ee-ut) A two-wheeled battle car pulled by horses.

colossal (kuh-LAH-sul) Gigantic.

deceased (dih-SEESD) Dead.

effigies (EH-fuh-jeez) Likenesses or images of a person.

Egyptologists (ee-jip-TAH-luh-jists) People who study the artifacts and culture of ancient Egypt.

funeral bier (FYOON-rul BEER) A frame or stand on which a coffin rests before being placed in a tomb.

granaries (GRAY-nuh-reez) Buildings for storing threshed grain.

hieroglyphs (HY-er-uh-glifs) Pictures or symbols used by the ancient Egyptians for writing.

lapis lazuli (LA-pis LA-zuh-lee) A rich blue semiprecious stone.

Middle Kingdom (MIH-dul KING-dum) A period of ancient Egyptian history from 2040 to 1640 BC.

mummification (muh-mih-fih-KAY-shun) The drying out of a dead body to prevent rotting.

natron (NAY-tron) A type of salt used for preserving bodies.

New Kingdom (NOO KING-dum) A period of ancient Egyptian history from 1550 to 1070 BC.

nutrients (NOO-tree-ents) Nourishing ingredients in food.

obelisks (AH-buh-lisks) Tall, slender, four-sided shafts of stone, that end with a pointed pyramidal top.

Old Kingdom (OHLD KING-dum) A period of ancient Egyptian history from 2649 to 2150 BC.

papyrus (puh-PY-rus) A form of paper made from the papyrus plant, which grows in the marshes beside the Nile River.

peasants (PEH-zentz) Members of a low social class who are farmers or farm laborers.

pharaoh (FER-oh) A ruler of ancient Egypt.

pyramid (PEER-uh-mid) A huge monument with a rectangular base and four triangular faces, built over or around a tomb.

Rosetta stone (roh-ZEH-tuh STOHN) A stone tablet, found at Rosetta in Egypt, with inscriptions in three different scripts that allowed scholars to break the code for ancient Egyptian hieroglyphs.

sarcophagus
(sar-KAH-fuh-gus) A stone coffin.

scribes (SKRYBZ) Public clerks
or writers.

shadoof (shuh-DOOF) A pole
with a bucket and counterweight,
used to raise water from a river.

shrine (SHRYN) A special
place built in honor of an
important person.

silt (SILT) Fine sand or clay.

sphinx (SFINKS) A mythical
beast of ancient Egypt that had
the body of a lion and the head of
a human, ram, or hawk.
Thousands of statues of sphinxes
were built in ancient Egypt, with
the greatest of them at Giza.

subterranean
(sub-tuh-RAY-nee-un)
Underground.

villas (VIH-luhz)
Large, luxurious country houses
of well-to-do people.

Index

Websites

Due to the changing nature of Internet links, PowerKids Press has developed an online list of websites related to the subject of this book. This site is updated regularly. Please use this link to access the list:
www.powerkidslinks.com/disc/egypt/